W9-AKA-035

FOR _____ _____

IN MEMORY OF _____ _____

FROM _____ _____

LA CROSSE COUNTY LIBRARY

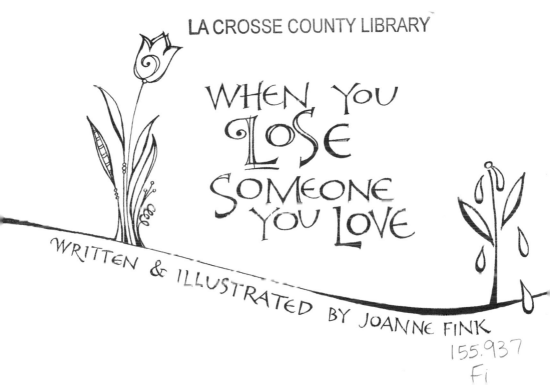

WHEN YOU LOSE SOMEONE YOU LOVE

WRITTEN & ILLUSTRATED BY JOANNE FINK

155.937
Fi

CompanionHouse Books™ is an imprint of Fox Chapel Publishing, Inc.

Director of Product Development and Editorial Operations: Christopher Reggio
Graphic Design: Angie Vangalis

Copyright © 2015, 2017 by Joanne Fink and Fox Chapel Publishing Company, Inc.,
East Petersburg, PA.

All rights reserved. No part of this book may be reproduced, stored in a retrieval system,
or transmitted in any form or by any means, electronic, mechanical, photocopying,
recording, or otherwise, without the prior written permission of Fox Chapel Publishing,
except for the inclusion of brief quotations in an acknowledged review.

ISBN 978-1-62008-231-7

CompanionHouse Books™
1970 Broad Street
East Petersburg, PA 17520
www.facebook.com/companionhousebooks

Printed and bound in China
20 19 18 17   2 4 6 8 10 9 7 5 3 1

THIS BOOK IS DEDICATED TO EVERYONE
WHO IS MOURNING THE LOSS
OF SOMEONE THEY LOVE...

Foreword

On August 3rd, my beloved husband, Andy Trattner, lay down to take a nap, had a heart attack while he was sleeping, and never woke up. He was only 53.

When we met at the end of my freshman year of college, his love changed my life; when he died, his loss shattered my world.

For several weeks after Andy died, I was so numb that I wasn't really functional. In fact, if I hadn't had to get up to get our children off to school, I don't think I would have ever gotten out of bed.

I met Andy when I was 18, and we were married for 29 years. He was my husband, my best friend, my business partner, and the father of our two children; his death has profoundly impacted every aspect of my life.

As an artist and writer, I process things by writing and drawing about them. The following pages are from the journal that I started keeping a few weeks after Andy died.

Keeping this journal has been cathartic for me. I am blessed to have incredibly supportive friends and family, and yet it has been hard for me to share with them how alone I feel, how sad I am, and how much I miss Andy. Instead, I've poured my soul into these pages.

I've discovered that grieving is like taking a journey toward an unknown destination against your will: it is incredibly difficult, heartbreaking, and time consuming—and there aren't any shortcuts.

At some point in our lives, most of us will experience the loss of someone we love and will need to deal with that loss in order to move on with our life's journey.

I have been deeply touched when those who have survived their own losses reached out to me with compassion and love. And although I am not very far along on my own journey, I wanted to share my journal in hopes that it will make your grief journey—or the journey of someone you love—a little easier.

Joanne Fink

WHEN YOU LOSE
SOMEONE YOU LOVE
YOU ARE
FOREVER CHANGED

THERE IS
A HOLE
IN YOUR
H·E·A·R·T

*which nothing
can fill.*

YOUR LIFE'S JOURNEY VEERS

NO CLUE ? ? WHERE YOU ARE HEADING ?

When you lose
someone you love

you feel
numb.

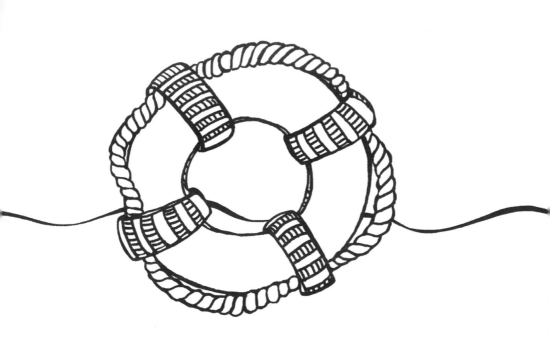

some days just surviving is ALL you can do.

WHEN YOU LOSE
SOMEONE YOU LOVE,

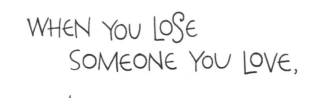

it sometimes
seems unfair
that the SUN is still
shining

because a

L·I·G·H·T

in your world

has gone out

and can
never be rekindled.

WHEN YOU LOSE SOMEONE YOU LOVE

EVERYTHING
SEEMS
DIS JOINTED

T·I·M·E
seems to move
at a different
p a c e   f o r   y o u

than for everyone else.

Sometimes you are so

unsteady you think THE GROUND HAS TURNED TO RUBBER

AND
YOU OFTEN
FEEL AFRAID
AND OVERWHELMED.

When you lose
someone you Love,
YOU SOMETIMES
FEEL ALONE
AND ABANDONED...

NOT ONLY BY THE PERSON YOU LOST,
BUT BY EVERYONE WHO
EXPRESSES SYMPATHY

AND THEN
GOES ON WITH THEIR LIVES...

WHEN YOUR WORLD WILL

never

BE
THE
SAME

AND YOUR

Heart
breaks

WHEN YOU
REALIZE

THAT YOU
CAN'T GLUE
THE BROKEN
PIECES OF
YOUR LIFE
BACK TOGETHER.

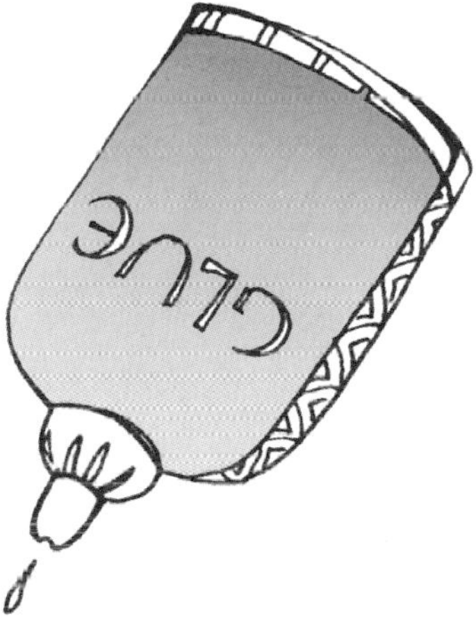

When you lose someone you love,
you sometimes get

REALLY ANGRY

with them for not
being here with you...

and then you get

REALLY ANGRY
WITH YOURSELF

for feeling that way.

WHEN YOU LOSE
SOMEONE YOU LOVE...

YOU BECOME MORE FEARFUL
BECAUSE YOU REALIZE

THERE ARE **NO** GUARANTEES IN LIFE

AND YOU WORRY ABOUT LOSING OTHER PEOPLE YOU LOVE

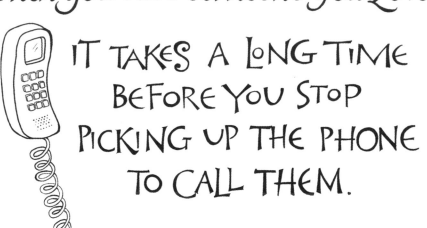

When you lose someone you Love,

IT TAKES A LONG TIME
BEFORE YOU STOP
PICKING UP THE PHONE
TO CALL THEM.

AND YOU'D GIVE ALMOST

Anything

IF YOU COULD JUST SEE THEM
ONE MORE TIME...

THERE ARE DAYS
YOU WONDER

HOW YOU CAN
GO ON WITHOUT THEM...

SOME DAYS
you don't want to

OTHER DAYS
YOU WANT TO
Live your best life
TO MAKE THEM
PROUD OF YOU.

When you lose
someone
you Love,

You can be OK
for hours or
even days at a time

and then totally lose it
for NO reason at all

OR MORE LIKELY
YOU PROBABLY LOST IT
BECAUSE YOU SAW
OR DID SOMETHING

YOU WANTED TO SHARE
WITH YOUR L♡VED ONE
AND REALIZED (AGAIN) THAT
they aren't there...

... AND THAT THEY AREN'T <u>EVER</u> COMING BACK.

MOST PEOPLE DON'T FULLY APPRECIATE

THE *Miracle* OF *life*

UNTIL THEY HELP BRING
A BABY INTO THE WORLD

AND MOST PEOPLE DON'T LEARN THAT

Love is Eternal

UNTIL THEY LOSE SOMEONE
THEY CHERISH AND REALIZE THAT...

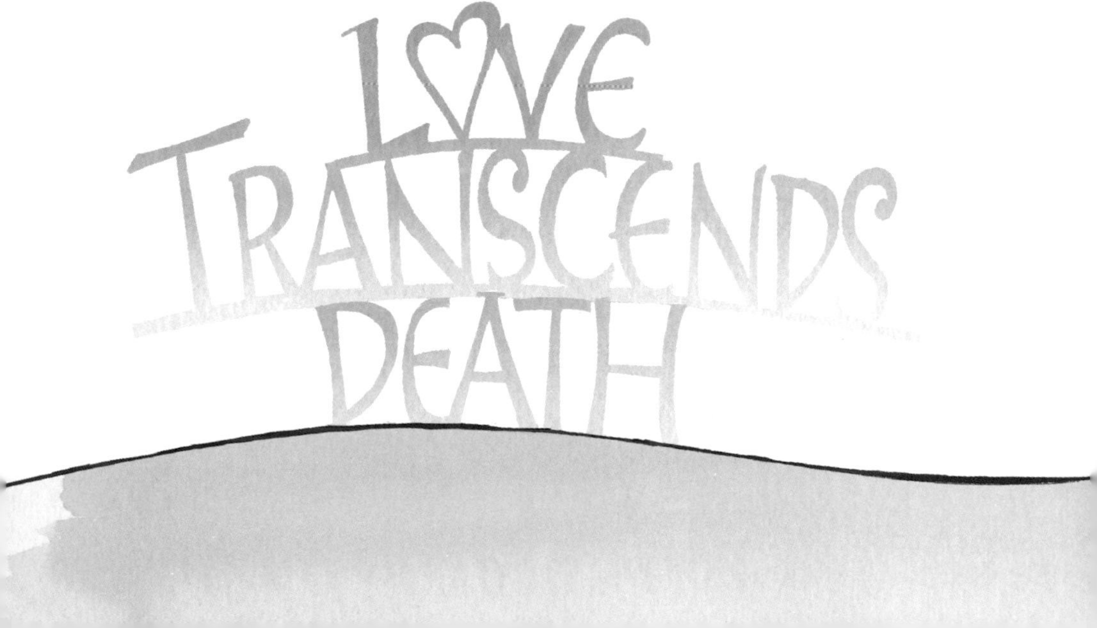
LOVE
TRANSCENDS
DEATH

YOU DON'T STOP LOVING
SOMEONE JUST BECAUSE
THEY AREN'T HERE ANYMORE.

waves of sadness over you unexpectedly can wash

making it Hard to BREATHE.

IT IS HARD TO SLEEP...
EVEN WEEKS AND
MONTHS LATER

SOMETIMES THE QUIET IS OVERWHELMING...

WHEN YOU LOSE SOMEONE YOU LOVE
YOU HAVE TO
rediscover yourself.

THE SEARCH FOR MEANING

Who am I?

Where am I headed?

What do I need to grow?

How can I become who I am supposed to be?

There
are days
you put a
mask on

and pretend
everything is "OK"
when someone asks
how you are...

WHEN YOU LOSE SOMEONE YOU LOVE

it is HARD *to go places*

ESPECIALLY PARTIES
AND CELEBRATIONS

without them.

YOU MISS A <u>LOT</u> OF
THINGS ABOUT THEM...
BUT YOU MISS THEIR HUGS,
AND HEARING THEM LAUGH,
MOST OF ALL

Birthdays

Vacations

Holidays

Weddings

Anniversaries

Dinner Parties

Reunions

Graduations

Celebrations

Family Get Togethers

The first few times you do something without your loved one are incredibly hard and usually require lots of tissues.

WHEN
YOU
LOSE
SOMEONE
YOU
LOVE

YOU DISCOVER
WHO YOUR TRUE
FRIENDS ARE...

AND HOW VERY
IMPORTANT FAMILY
& FRIENDS CAN BE.

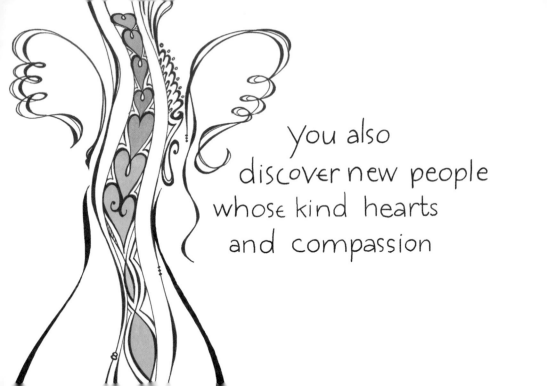

You also
discover new people
whose kind hearts
and compassion

touch you
in ways you would never
have dreamed before your
loved one died.

When you lose someone you love
you appreciate photos of them
more than you ever
dreamed possible...

and you wish you had a recording
of their voice saying "I love you"
so you could listen to it
whenever you want.

You enjoy hearing stories about them...

especially ones you've never heard before...

IT CAN HELP TO REMINISCE
WITH FRIENDS & FAMILY
WHO SHARE YOUR LOSS

WHEN YOU LOSE SOMEONE YOU LOVE

YOU BEGIN
YOUR LIFE'S
JOURNEY ANEW...

... AND YOU LEARN TO CARRY THE MOST MEANINGFUL PARTS

memories are a blessing

WHEN YOU LOSE
SOMEONE
YOU LOVE,

Everything CHANGES

Even the things you wish
would remain the same.

You remember all
the things which
make them so special...

and you look for ways
to keep their memory
vibrantly, alive.

WHEN YOU LOSE SOMEONE YOU LOVE,

YOU LEARN THAT
YOU CAN SURVIVE THE
UNIMAGINABLE...

WHEN YOU LOSE SOMEONE YOU LOVE
IT HELPS TO LOOK
UP AT THE STARS
AND IMAGINE
THAT THE LIGHT OF
YOUR LOVED ONE'S S·O·U·L

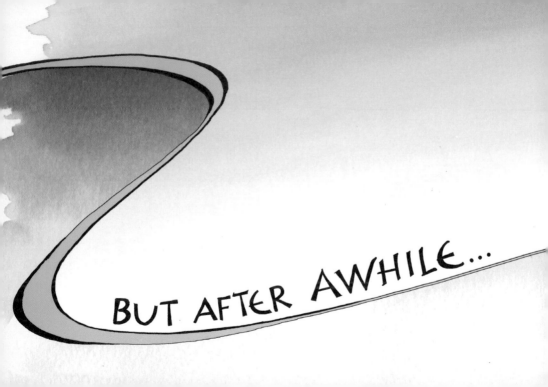

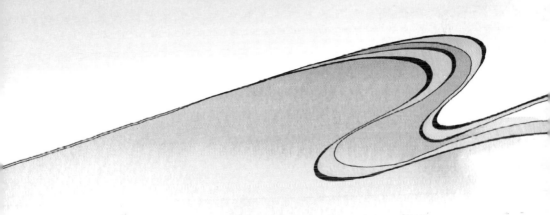

IT DOES GET
EASIER TO BEAR

WHEN YOU LOSE
SOMEONE YOU LOVE

YOU CARRY THEIR
MEMORY
INSIDE YOUR HEART
Forever

Epilogue

It has been almost five years since I wrote the first draft of this book. Although there are still days I feel profoundly dysfunctional, fortunately those days occur less frequently. I think this is true for our children, too; they both occasionally have bad days, but we have all regained some equilibrium and a sense of purpose. Two and a half years ago, I raised funds to self-publish the first edition of this book through Kickstarter. I am immensely grateful to the 449 Kickstarter supporters who committed resources to help me share my story. Thank you for believing in my dream! My dream has now evolved: I want to change the culture of grief support in America by developing products aimed at comforting those who are grieving and educating their friends and family about ways to show support. To focus on this endeavor, I've partnered with Fox Chapel Publishing to publish this edition of *When You Lose Someone You Love*.

Andy was an awesome dad, and nothing was more important to him than our children. I marvel as they continue to grow into grounded, caring individuals, and I take joy in knowing how very proud their father would be of them. Our son inherited some of Andy's best qualities: intelligence, stage presence, humor, and a deep sense of integrity. Our daughter continually strives to become the person she knows her dad wants her to be. While I process things by putting pen to paper, Samantha processes her grief musically. It took her three years to write the song "Legacy," an amazing tribute to her dad. My favorite lyrics:

> *You're everything I see; not just a memory...*
> *You'll live on through me; I am your legacy.*

Sam has recorded nine other original songs and is about to publish her first CD, *Listen*, in memory of her dad.

Andy was committed to making a difference in the world. I celebrate his life and honor his commitment by sharing stories about him and supporting things I know he valued. One way I do this is by donating a portion of the proceeds from this book to the Modern Widows Club (www.modernwidowsclub.com), a nonprofit organization that mentors widows around the globe. I am honored to help support MWC's important work and hope you will let others know about this wonderful organization.

When you lose someone you love, you often feel lost and alone and aren't sure how to get your life back on track. Joining MWC made a big difference in my life: I felt an immediate connection with the widows I met through MWC, and am deeply grateful for the support we provide to one another in person and online.

If you have recently lost someone you love, please know that there is no time frame for grief. Everyone grieves at their own pace and in their own way; each person's grief journey is different. There is a chasm that separates those who have experienced profound loss from those who haven't, and once you've crossed it, you're forever changed—but you are not alone. It really helps to be with people who have also experienced loss and can understand, at least on some level, what you are going through. If you would like to connect with others who have lost someone they love, there are resources that might interest you on my website, www.zenspirations.com, and on my "*When You Lose Someone You Love*" Facebook page.

There has not been a single day when I have not thought about Andy. His death has taught me so much about life—I have grown in ways that I never would have imagined before he died. I know I am a more compassionate, caring person today because I understand firsthand how devastating it is to lose someone you love dearly.

With sympathy for your loss,

Joanne Fink

WS. 10/17

Love is Eternal

Additional copies of

WHEN YOU LOSE SOMEONE YOU LOVE

available through
www.foxchapelpublishing.com
www.zenspirations.com

A portion of the proceeds benefits Modern Widows Club.

www.facebook.com/companionhousebooks